Contents

Copyright ©2020.EMILY ROBERT.

All rights reserved. No part of this publication may be reproduced, distributed, or transmitted in any form or by any means, including photocopying, recording, or other electronic or mechanical methods, without the prior written permission of the publisher, except in the case of brief quotations embodied in critical reviews and certain other noncommercial uses permitted by copyright law.

INTRODUCTION

One seed-to-seed life cycle for an annual can occur in as little as a month in some species, though most last several months. Oilseed rapa can go from seed-to-seed in about five weeks under a bank of fluorescent lamps. This style of growing is often used in classrooms for education. Many desert annuals are therophytes, because their seed-to-seed life cycle is only weeks and they spend most of the year as seeds to survive dry conditions.

Perennials typically grow structures that allow them to adapt to living from one year to the next through a form of vegetative reproduction rather than seeding. These structures include bulbs, tubers, woody crowns, rhizomes plus others. They might have specialized stems or crowns that allow them to survive periods of dormancy over cold or dry seasons during the year. Annuals produce seeds to continue the species as a new generation while the growing season is suitable, and the seeds survive over the cold or dry period to begin growth when the conditions are again suitable.

Smart bulb planting starts at the garden center with high-quality bulbs. Look for those that are plump and firm. It's typically best to avoid bulbs that are soft and mushy or have mold growing on them. Also look for big bulbs; the bigger they are, the more they generally bloom compared to smaller bulbs of the same variety.

CHAPTER ONE

Annual Plants

An annual plant is a plant that completes its life cycle, from germination to the production of seeds, within one growing season, and then dies. The length of growing seasons and period in which they take place vary according to geographical location, and may not correspond to the four traditional seasonal divisions of the year. With respect to the traditional seasons annual plants are generally categorized into summer annuals and winter annuals. Summer annuals germinate during spring or early summer and mature by autumn of the same year. Winter annuals germinate during the autumn and mature during the spring or summer of the following calendar year.

Cultivation

In cultivation, many food plants are, or are grown as, annuals, including virtually all domesticated grains. Some perennials and biennials are grown in gardens as annuals for convenience, particularly if they are not considered cold hardy for the local climate. Carrot, celery and parsley are true biennials (divarsiya) that are usually grown as annual crops for their edible roots, petioles and leaves, respectively. Tomato, sweet potato and bell pepper are tender perennials usually grown as annuals. Ornamental perennials commonly grown as annuals are impatiens, mirabilis, wax begonia, snapdragon, pelargonium, coleus and petunia.

Winter

Winter annuals germinate in autumn or winter, live through the winter, then bloom in winter or spring. The plants grow and bloom during the cool season when most other plants are dormant or other annuals are in seed form waiting for warmer weather to germinate. Winter annuals die after flowering and setting seed. The seeds germinate in the autumn or winter when the soil temperature is cool.

Winter annuals typically grow low to the ground, where they are usually sheltered from the coldest nights by snow cover, and make use of warm periods in winter for growth when the snow melts. Some common winter annuals include henbit, deadnettle, chickweed, and winter cress.

Winter annuals are important ecologically, as they provide vegetative cover that prevents soil erosion during winter and early spring when no other cover exists and they provide fresh vegetation for animals and birds that feed on them. Although they are often considered to be weeds in gardens, this viewpoint is not always necessary, as most of them die when the soil temperature warms up again in early to late spring when other plants are still dormant and have not yet leafed out.

Even though they do not compete directly with cultivated plants, sometimes winter annuals are considered a pest in commercial agriculture, because they can be hosts for insect pests or fungal diseases (ovary smut – Microbotryum sp) which attack crops being cultivated. The property that they prevent the soil from drying out can also be problematic for commercial agriculture.

Perennial plant

A perennial plant or simply perennial is a plant that lives more than two years. The term (per- + -ennial, "through the years") is often used to differentiate a plant from shorter-lived annuals and biennials. The term is also widely used to distinguish plants with little or no woody growth from trees and shrubs, which are also technically perennials.

Perennials—especially small flowering plants—that grow and bloom over the spring and summer, die back every autumn and winter, and then return in the spring from their rootstock, are known as herbaceous perennials. However, depending on the rigors of local climate, a plant that is a perennial in its native habitat, or in a milder garden, may be treated by a gardener as an annual and planted out every year, from seed, from cuttings or from divisions. Tomato vines, for example, live several years in their natural tropical/subtropical habitat but are grown as annuals in temperate regions because they don't survive the winter.

There is also a class of evergreen, or non-herbaceous, perennials, including plants like Bergenia which retain a mantle of leaves throughout the year. An intermediate class of plants is known as subshrubs, which retain a vestigial woody structure in winter, e.g. Penstemon. The local climate may dictate whether plants are treated as shrubs or perennials. For instance, many varieties of Fuchsia are shrubs in warm regions, but in colder temperate climates may be cut to the ground every year as a result of winter frosts.

Life cycle and structure

Perennial plants can be short-lived (only a few years) or they can be long-lived, as are some woody plants like trees. They include a wide assortment of plant groups from ferns and liverworts to the highly diverse flowering plants like orchids and grasses.

Plants that flower and fruit only once and then die are termed monocarpic or semelparous. However, most perennials are polycarpic (or iteroparous), flowering over many seasons in their lifetime.

Many perennials have developed specialized features that allow them to survive extreme climatic and environmental conditions. Some have adapted to survive hot and dry conditions or cold temperatures. Those plants tend to invest many resources into their adaptations and often do not flower and set seed until after a few years of growth. Many perennials produce relatively large seeds, which can have an advantage, with larger seedlings produced after germination that can better compete with other plants. Some annuals produce many more seeds per plant in one season, while some (polycarpic) perennials are not under the same pressure to produce large numbers of seeds but can produce seeds over many years.

Dividing perennial plants is something that gardeners do around the months of September and October. The point of doing the division at this time is to allow approximately 6 weeks for adequate root growth prior to the ground reaching a freezing temperature. Due to the leaves falling from trees, as well as the excessive amount of rain received in most places during the fall weeks, the ground has adequate moisture for rapid growth. Each type of plant must be separated differently; for example, plants with large root systems like oriental grasses can be cut by knives and pulled apart. However, plants such as Irises have a root system known as a Rhizomes, these root systems should be planted with the bulb of the plant just above ground level, with leaves from the following year showing. The point of dividing perennials is to increase the amount of a single breed of plant in your garden. The more you divide your perennial plants every year, the more vast your garden will grow

Growth

In warmer and more favorable climates, perennials grow continuously. In seasonal climates, their growth is limited to the growing season.

In some species, perennials retain their foliage all year round; these are evergreen perennials. Other plants are deciduous perennials, for example, in temperate regions a perennial plant may grow and bloom during the warm part of the year, with the foliage dying back in the winter. In many parts of the world, seasonality is expressed as wet and dry periods rather than warm and cold periods, and deciduous perennials lose their leaves in the dry season.

With their roots protected below ground in the soil layer, perennial plants are notably tolerant of wildfire. Herbaceous perennials are also able to tolerate the extremes of cold in temperate and Arctic winters, with less sensitivity than trees or shrubs.

Perennial plants can also be differentiated from annuals and biennials in that perennials have the ability to remain dormant over long periods of time and then continue growth and reproduction. The meristem of perennial plants communicates with the hormones produced due to environmental situations (i.e. seasons), reproduction, and stage of development to begin and halt the ability to grow or flower. There is also a distinction between the ability to grow and actual task of growth. For example, most trees regain the ability to grow in the midst of winter but do not initiate physical growth until the spring and summer months. The start of dormancy can be seen in perennials plants through withering flowers, loss of leaves on trees, and halting of reproduction in both flowering and budding plants.

The growth of a deciduous perennial plant is studied to the point where we can make basic assumptions. The first assumption is not only about the daily net photosynthetic rate of a plant increasing, but also how it saturates with the size of the plant. Secondly, while the production of the plant is discarded, the stored material will be used during the next season to keep it growing. Finally, the plant maximizes its lifetime by choosing the best growth schedule within each season and also allocating resources between reproduction for the year and the storage for next year. Perennial planting in general have a low storage, low growth rate, and a short growing season. When it comes to the optimal phenology of a plant, its quantity can be measured in two specific ways:

firstly, by its productivity, which is the growth rate of the plant and secondly, by its stability, the survival storage it requires to survive through the season.

Although most of humanity is fed by the re-sowing of the seeds of annual grain crops, (either naturally or by the manual efforts of man), perennial crops provide numerous benefits. Perennial plants often have deep, extensive root systems which can hold soil to prevent erosion, capture dissolved nitrogen before it can contaminate ground and surface water, and out-compete weeds (reducing the need for herbicides). These potential benefits of perennials have resulted in new attempts to increase the seed yield of perennial species, which could result in the creation of new perennial grain crops. Some examples of new perennial crops being developed are perennial rice and intermediate wheatgrass.

Perennial plants dominate many natural ecosystems on land and in fresh water, with only a very few (e.g. Zostera) occurring in shallow sea water. Herbaceous perennial plants are particularly dominant in conditions too fire-prone for trees and shrubs, e.g., most plants on prairies and steppes are perennials; they are also dominant on tundra too cold for tree growth. Nearly all forest plants are perennials, including the trees and shrubs.

Perennial plants are usually better competitors than annual plants, especially under stable, resource-poor conditions. This is due to the development of larger root systems which can access water and soil nutrients deeper in the soil and to earlier emergence in the spring.

Perennial flowers

• Dahlia

• Gulmohur

• Hibiscus

• Kniphofia

Perennial fruits

• Apple

- Apricot

- Avocado

- Banana

- Blackcurrant

- Blueberry

- Blackberry

- Currant

- Feijoa

- Grape

- Kiwi fruit

- Japanese wineberry

- Pear

- Persimmon

- Pineapple

- Plum

- Pomegranate

• Raspberries

• Strawberry

• Strawberry tree

• Tomato

The following perennial plants are used as herbs:

• Agastache

• Alfalfa

• Althaea officinalis (marshmallow)

• Basil, many varieties: African blue, East Indian

• Chives

• Fennel

• Ferula

• Garlic

• Ginger

• Hops - Humulus

• Hyssop

• Horseradish

• Lavender

• Lemon balm

• Mint

• Onions, many varieties: potato onions, shallots, Egyptian onions, Japanese bunching onions, Welsh onions, Chinese leeks

• Oregano

• Piper nigrum (black pepper)

• Rosemary

• Sage

• Thyme

• Valerian

• White horehound - Marrubium vulgare

• Yarrow - Achillea millefolium

Many vegetable plants can grow as perennials in tropical climates, but die in cold weather. Some of the more completely perennial vegetables are:

- Allium tricoccum

- Asparagus

- Broccoli: nine star

- Chives

- Colocasia esculenta

- Globe artichoke

- Apios americana ground Nut

- Jerusalem artichoke

- Konjac

- Leek

- Milkweed (Asclepias)

- New Zealand spinach

- Potato

- Radicchio or a.k.a. Italian chicory

- Rhubarb

- Siberian pea tree (Caragana arborescens)

- Sorrel

- Rakkyo

- Sea kale

- Collard greens

- Mustard greens

- Turnip greens

- Kale

- Sweet potato

- Taro

- Watercress

Bulb

In botany, a bulb is structurally a short stem with fleshy leaves or leaf bases that function as food storage organs during dormancy. (In gardening, plants with other kinds of storage organ are also called "ornamental bulbous plants" or just "bulbs".)

A bulb's leaf bases, also known as scales, generally do not support leaves, but contain food reserves to enable the plant to survive adverse conditions. At the center of the bulb is a vegetative growing point or an unexpanded flowering shoot. The base is formed by a reduced stem, and plant growth occurs from this basal plate. Roots emerge from the underside of the base, and new stems and leaves from the upper side. Tunicate bulbs have dry, membranous outer scales that protect the continuous lamina of fleshy scales. Species in the genera Allium, Hippeastrum, Narcissus, and Tulipa all have tunicate bulbs. Non-tunicate bulbs, such as Lilium and Fritillaria species, lack the protective tunic and have looser scales.

Bulbous plant species cycle through vegetative and reproductive growth stages; the bulb grows to flowering size during the vegetative stage and the plant flowers during the reproductive stage. Certain environmental conditions are needed to trigger the transition from one stage to the next, such as the shift from a cold winter to spring. Once the flowering period is over, the plant enters a foliage period of about six weeks during which time the plant absorbs nutrients from the soil and energy from the sun for setting flowers for the next year. Bulbs dug up before the foliage period is completed will not bloom the following year but then should flower normally in subsequent years.

Plants that form bulbs

Plants that form underground storage organs, including bulbs as well as tubers and corms, are called geophytes. Some epiphytic orchids (family Orchidaceae) form above-ground storage organs called pseudobulbs, that superficially resemble bulbs.

Nearly all plants that form true bulbs are monocotyledons, and include:

• Amaryllis, Crinum, Hippeastrum, Narcissus, and several other members of the amaryllis family

Amaryllidaceae. This includes onion, garlic, and other alliums, members of the Amaryllid subfamily Allioideae.

• Lily, tulip, and many other members of the lily family Liliaceae.

• Two groups of Iris species, family Iridaceae: subgenus Xiphium (the "Dutch" irises) and subgenus Hermodactyloides (the miniature "rock garden" irises).

Oxalis, in the family Oxalidaceae, is the only dicotyledon genus that produces true bulbs

Bulbil

A bulbil is a small bulb, and may also be called a bulblet, bulbet, or bulbel.

Small bulbs can develop or propagate a large bulb. If one or several moderate-sized bulbs form to replace the original bulb, they are called renewal bulbs. Increase bulbs are small bulbs that develop either on each of the leaves inside a bulb, or else on the end of small underground stems connected to the original bulb.

Some lilies, such as the tiger lily Lilium lancifolium, form small bulbs, called bulbils, in their leaf axils. Several members of the onion family, Alliaceae, including Allium sativum (garlic), form bulbils in their flower heads, sometimes as the flowers fade, or even instead of the flowers (which is a form of apomixis). The so-called tree onion (Allium × proliferum) forms small onions which are large enough for pickling.

Some ferns, such as the hen-and-chicken fern, produce new plants at the tips of the fronds' pinnae that are sometimes referred to as bulbils.

CHAPTER TWO

The answer to "what is an annual plant" is, generally speaking, a plant which dies within one growing season; in other words — an annual plant cycle. Let's see if we can sort it out. Hardy annuals – Hardy annuals fall into the general definition above but do not need to be started inside. Sowing of hardy annuals can take place directly in the garden soil since they are more tolerant of light frosts. A few examples of hardy annuals for the garden are:

Larkspur

Growing larkspur flowers (Consolida sp.) provides tall, early season color in the spring landscape. Once you learn how to grow larkspur, you will likely include them in the garden year after year. Deciding when to plant larkspurs will depend somewhat on your location. Once established, however, larkspur flower care is simple and basic. Learning how to grow larkspur is easier if you are somewhat familiar with local weather patterns, although, of course, there is no guarantee that the weather will cooperate with your gardening schedule.

How to Grow Larkspur Flowers

Most annual larkspur plants are grown from seeds, though planting larkspur seeds can be challenging. When planting larkspur seeds, they must have a cold period before germination. This can be accomplished before planting the seeds, after planting the seeds in peat pots, or after sowing the seeds directly in the flower bed. The most reliable method of chilling larkspur seeds before planting can be done in the refrigerator. Chill protected seeds for two weeks prior to planting. Place seeds in a zip lock sandwich bag and include some damp perlite to provide moisture. Planting larkspur seeds in peat pots or other plantable containers will also work. If there is a building, basement or cold room where temperatures will remain between 40 and 50 F. (4-10 C.), plant them in moist soil and chill them there for two weeks. Keep in mind that larkspur seeds often will not germinate at temps above 65 F. (18 C.).

Learning when to plant larkspurs that have been chilled requires knowing when the first frost date occurs in your area. Planting larkspur seeds should be done early enough before frost for them to begin developing a root system to hold them over through winter. After germination, when seedlings in peat pots have two sets of true leaves, they may be moved into the garden or a permanent container. Growing larkspur flowers do not like to be moved, so plant seeds into their permanent location. Spring planting of larkspur seeds can be done, but flowers may not reach their full potential.

Larkspur Flower Care

Annual larkspur flower care includes thinning sprouting seedlings 10 to 12 inches apart so that each new growing larkspur has enough room to grow and develop its own root system. Staking the tall plants is another aspect of larkspur flower care. Provide support when they are young, with a stake that can accommodate the potential 6 to 8 foot growth. These plants will also require occasional watering during periods of drought. Growing larkspur flowers centered in containers can be part of an eye catching display. Use containers that won't topple under the weight and height of the growing larkspur flowers. Larkspurs in the garden will often self-seed and can provide more additional larkspur flowers for the following year.

Bachelor Button Flowers

Bachelor buttons (Centaurea cyanus) offer many uses in the landscape, as this European native naturalizes easily in most parts of the United States. Attractive flowers, now in shades of red, white and pink are available in addition to the traditional blue color of bachelor button flowers. Combine red, white and blue varieties for a patriotic display on the 4th of July. Plant bachelor button flowers in borders, rock gardens and sunny areas where they can spread and naturalize. Frilly, showy flowers grow on multi-branching stems, which may reach 2 to 3 feet (60-90 cm.). Bachelor button flowers are reseeding annuals and blooms may be single or double. Once planted, you will be growing bachelor buttons year after year as the reseed freely.

How to Grow Bachelor Buttons Growing bachelor buttons can be as simple as broadcasting or planting seeds outdoors in spring. Seeds may be started earlier inside and moved to the garden when frost danger has passed. Care of bachelor buttons plants requires watering to get them started and little else for continued bachelor buttons care. Once established, the flower is drought resistant and will self-seed for a continuing display in coming years. Bachelor buttons care can include deadheading the plants to prevent prolific self-seeding. This can control next year's spread of the cornflower. Weeding out sprigs growing in unwanted areas may also be included in bachelor buttons care and maintenance.

Half-hardy annuals

Half-hardy annuals are started indoors four to eight weeks before the last frost. These annuals are not frost hardy and cannot be planted until all danger of frost has passed. They fall into the same definition as other annuals as they germinate, grow, flower and die all in a single year. Some half-hardy perennials are grown like annuals. These include:

Dahlias

Planting dahlias is not very difficult. as they are either grown from seed or tubers. Dahlias come in a variety of colors and sizes, and are quite versatile in the garden. Nothing makes your summer garden stand out more than these colorful blooms. Keep reading to learn more about how to plant dahlia flowers.

How to Plant Dahlias

First time dahlia growers often wonder when to plant dahlias. Planting dahlia tubers can be done in the spring. If you start planting dahlias from seed, you should start them indoors or directly in the garden once the temperatures are warm enough. Dahlias will typically germinate in five to seven days. Once they germinate, you will want to keep an eye on them and make sure that they are watered enough, but don't soak the soil. You can also purchase tubers or divide existing dahlia plants and use them for planting dahlia tubers – dig up the root ball of the dahlia and separate the tubers so you can transplant them. Make sure each of the tubers has one eye. Place them about an inch (2.5 cm.) into the soil. Make sure you are planting dahlias where there is enough sunlight but also some shade. They like five to six hours of sunlight each day, but that's about it. You should see life from the tuber you planted within a week.

Gazania

If you're looking for a showy annual bloom in the sunny garden or the container, something you can just plant and forget about, try growing Gazanias. In USDA hardiness zones 9-11, Gazanias perform as herbaceous, tender perennials.

Care of Gazania flowers is limited and often non-existent if you have neither the time nor the inclination to care for them. Botanically called Gazania rigens, treasure flowers is a more common name. The plant is often referred to as the African daisy (though not to be confused with Osteospermum African daisies). The South African native often trails along the ground. In areas where it is hardy, landscapers use this plant in combination with other low growers as an ornamental ground cover to edge lawns or even replace parts of them. Learning how to prune trailing Gazanias allows the home gardener to use Gazania treasure flowers in this manner. When growing Gazanias, expect the plant to reach 6 to 18 inches (15-46 cm.) in height and about the same in spread as it trails on the ground. A clumping mound of grass-like foliage produces Gazania treasure flowers. This easy-to-grow bloom is tolerant of poor, dry or sandy soil. Heat and salty spray don't deter its growth or beautiful blossoms either, making it a perfect specimen for oceanfront growing.

Growing Gazanias bloom in vivid shades of red, yellow, orange, pink and white and can be two tone or multi-colored. Showy blooms appear in early summer through early fall on this annual wildflower. Care of Gazania flowers is simple once they're planted and established in the garden.

Geraniums can be removed from the soil prior to the first frost and overwintered inside while dahlias and begonias are dug up and their root systems are stored in a cool, dry area until it's time to start them for next year's growing season. Other annual garden plants may be grown as perennials. Depending upon the climate in certain geographic regions, a plant may act as an annual or a perennial. For example, warmer areas of the United States, such as the South, cause some annual plants (like mums or pansies) or tender perennials (like snapdragons) to have a shorter growth season, as they prefer cooler temps. Likewise, cooler regions may extend the life of these plants, allowing them to flourish for more than one season, more like a perennial or a biennial.

List of Annual Plants

A complete list of annual plants would be fairly extensive and does depend on your USDA plant hardiness zone. Most traditional bedding plants available in your area are considered to be annuals. Most vegetables (or garden fruit like tomatoes) are grown as annuals. Other common annuals grown for their flowers or foliage include

Amaranth

Though the amaranth plant is typically grown as a decorative flower in North America and Europe, it is, in fact, an excellent food crop that is grown in many parts of the world. Growing amaranth for food is fun and interesting, and adds a little bit of something different to your vegetable garden.

What is Amaranth?

The amaranth plant is a grain and greens crop plant. The plant develops long flowers, which can be upright or trailing depending on the variety. The flowers are used to produce the amaranth grain, while the leaves can be used as amaranth greens.

Varieties of Amaranth as Food

When growing amaranth for food, it is best to select varieties of amaranth that work well as a food crop. If you want to grow amaranth as a grain, some amaranth varieties to consider include: Amaranthus caudatus Amaranthus cruentus Amaranthus hypochondriacus Amaranthus retroflexus If you want to grow amaranth plants as a leafy greens, some amaranth varieties best suited to this include:

Amaranthus cruentus Amaranthus blitum Amaranthus dubius Amaranthus tricolor Amaranthus viridis

How to Plant Amaranth

Amaranth plants grow well in average to rich, well-draining soil with equal amounts of nitrogen and phosphorus. Like many vegetable crops, they need at least five hours of sunlight a day to do well. While they grows best in moist but well drained soil, they will tolerate somewhat dry soil too. Amaranth seeds are very fine, so generally, the seeds are sprinkled over a prepared area after the risk of last frost has passed. Amaranth seeds can be started indoors as well about three to four weeks before the last frost date. Once the amaranth seeds have sprouted, they should be thinned to about 18 inches (46 cm.) apart.

How to Grow Amaranth

Once established, amaranth needs little care. It is more tolerant of drought than most other leafy vegetable and will tolerate a wider range of soils than other grain crops. How to Harvest Amaranth Harvesting Amaranth Leaves The leaves on an amaranth plant can be used at any time. Just like other greens, the smaller the leaf, the more tender it is, but larger leaves have a more developed flavor.

Harvesting Amaranth Grains

If you would like to harvest the amaranth grain, allow the plant to go to flower. Flowering amaranth plants can still have their leaves harvested to eat, but you may find that the flavor changes after the amaranth plant flowers. Once the flowers have developed, let the amaranth flowers grow fully and watch carefully for the first few flowers to start dying back or browning a bit. At this time, cut all of the flowers off the amaranth plant and place them in paper bags to dry the rest of the way. Once the amaranth flowers are dry, the flowers must be threshed (basically beaten) either over a cloth or inside a bag to release the amaranth grains. Use water or wind to separate the amaranth grains from their chaff.

Baby's Breath

We're all familiar with the baby's breath plant (Gypsophila paniculata), from bridal bouquets to cut flower arrangements that use the small, delicate white flowers, fresh or dried, to fill in around larger blooms. But did you know that baby's breath flowers can grow easily in your garden? You can learn how to dry your own baby's breath for making arrangements at home and to share with friends simply by growing baby's breath flowers in your garden. This plant may be annual or perennial, and baby's breath flowers grow in rose, pink and white and may have single or double blooms. Double blooming baby's breath plants have been grafted, so take care to cut above the graft union.

How to Grow Baby's Breath?

Growing baby's breath is simple and you'll likely find it a useful garden specimen. Learning how to grow baby's breath can be a lucrative hobby, especially if you sell it to florists and others who make professional arrangements. Growing baby's breath in a full sun area is relatively simple if the soil pH is right. The baby's breath plant likes an alkaline or sweet soil. Soil should also be well-draining. If your baby's breath plant does not perform well, take a soil test to determine the soil's alkalinity. Start baby's breath flowers in the garden from seeds, cuttings or tissue cultured plants.

How to Dry Your Own Baby's Breath

Reaching 12 to 18 inches (30.5-46 cm.) at maturity, you can harvest and learn how to dry your own baby's breath flowers. When cutting to dry flowers of the baby's breath plant, choose stems with just half of the flowers in bloom while others are only buds. Don't use stems with browning flowers. Re-cut stems of the baby's breath under warm running water. Bundle five to seven stems together with twine or a rubber band. Hang these upside down in a dark, warm and well-ventilated room. Check the drying flowers after five days. When flowers are papery to the touch, they are ready for use in a dried arrangement. If they do not have the papery feel after five days, allow more time, checking every couple of days. Now that you've learned how to grow baby's breath and how to dry it, include it as a border in your garden. If it does well, check with local florists to see if they are interested in purchasing some of the flowers you've perfected in your garden.

NOTE: This plant is considered a noxious weed in some parts of the U.S. and Canada. Before planting anything in your garden, it is always important to check if a plant is invasive in your particular area.

Cosmos

Cosmos plants (Cosmos bipinnatus) are an essential for many summer gardens, reaching varying heights and in many colors, adding frilly texture to the flower bed. Growing cosmos is simple and cosmos flower care is easy and rewarding when single or double blooms appear on stems reaching 1 to 4 feet. Cosmos plants may be featured at the back of a descending garden or in the middle of an island garden. Taller varieties may need staking if not planted in an area protected from wind. Planting cosmos flowers results in many uses of the specimen, such as cut flowers for the indoor display and backgrounds for other plants.

Cosmos can even be used as screens to hide unsightly elements in the landscape.

How to Grow Cosmos Flowers

When planting cosmos flowers, locate them in soil that has not been heavily amended. Hot dry conditions, along with poor to average soil are optimum conditions for growing cosmos. Cosmos plants are usually grown from seed. Scatter seeds of the cosmos onto a bare area in the location where you wish to have growing cosmos. Once planted, this annual flower self-seeds and will provide more cosmos flowers in the area for years to come. Daisy-like flowers of the cosmos plant appear atop tall stems with lacy foliage. Cosmos flower care can include deadheading of flowers as they appear. This practice forces growth lower on the flower stem and results in a stronger plant with more flowers. Cosmos flower care can include cutting flowers for indoor use, achieving the same affect on the growing cosmos plant.

More than 20 varieties of cosmos plants exist, both annual and perennial varieties. Two annual varieties of cosmos plants are primarily grown in the U.S. Cosmos bipinnatus, called the Mexican aster and Cosmos sulphureus, yellow cosmos. Yellow cosmos is somewhat shorter and more compact than the commonly used Mexican aster. Another interesting variety is Cosmos atrosanguineus, the chocolate cosmos. If there are no cosmos to self-seed in your flower bed, get some started this year. Direct sow this frilly flower into a bare area of the bed that will benefit from tall, colorful, easy care blooms.

Evening Primrose

The evening primrose plant is one of the few native wildflowers in North America. As the name suggests, the yellow evening primrose blooms at night. It produces lovely yellow flowers from May to July. It is considered to have a wide array of medicinal uses from relieving headaches and inducing labor to curing baldness and as a treatment for laziness. All parts if the evening primrose plant can also be eaten. The leaves are eaten like leaves and the roots are eaten like potatoes.

Growing Evening Primrose

Part of the reason that many people regard this plant as a weed is that growing evening primrose is extremely easy to do. The yellow evening primrose plant is happiest in dry open areas similar to the open meadows where they thrive in the wild. Simply spread the seeds where you would like them to grow and as long as it is not too wet, the yellow evening primrose will happily grow. It is a biennial that will reseed itself wherever you plant it, but it is not very invasive and will remain well behaved in your flower beds. Transplanting an evening primrose plant will probably not succeed, so you are better off planting them from seed.

Perennial Plants

Agastache

Agastache plants bring hummingbirds, bees, and butterflies to your garden with their tall spikes of long-lasting, tubular blooms. Also known as Hummingbird Mint and Anise Hyssop, these versatile perennials are excellent for borders and container plantings, either in full or part sun. They grow best in well-drained soils, and once established are considered to be both drought and heat tolerant. Agastache leaves have a bold, aromatic scent, which makes them great for bouquets

Ajuga

Ajuga, also known as "Carpet Bugleweed," is a small, spreading evergreen plant that many gardeners love. Its beauty lies in its waxy, weed-suppressing foliage that spreads eagerly, even in the deep shade where grass won't grow. Ajuga is available in a range of colors and grows to be 6 -12" in height, making it an ideal ground cover for creating a "blooming carpet". Best of all, Ajuga is deer resistant and low-maintenance, and can even be used for erosion control.

Astilbe

Astilbes are excellent at creating soft, colorful displays underneath trees, in low light corners, or in shady borders. These low-maintenance perennial plants make lovely foliage, and in late spring, send up plume-like flowers in a host of rich, glowing colors. Some are even sweetly fragrant. Their deeply-cut leaves and feathery blooms also offer a great way to add texture and interest to container gardens and cut-flower arrangements

Daylily

Beginners learn quickly, and the master gardeners already know, that an investment in Daylilies always pays off. Attractive foliage complements flowers that bloom in late spring to early summer, available in a wide range of warm, sunny colors. Look for Reblooming Daylilies for beautiful blooms during in late spring, plus a grand finale of flowers just before fall. Excellent for mass planting, Daylilies are the key to filling in a low-maintenance garden with color and texture.

Euphorbia

Euphorbia is an easy to grow and hardy perennial. Also known as Spurge, this plant naturalizes to form an excellent, deer-resistant ground cover that provides early spring color and texture. Use low-growing Euphorbia in border plantings and to add excitement to rock gardens.

Delphinium

A cottage garden favorite, Delphiniums boast spikes of brightly-colored flowers in cool colors. The plants form mounds of dark green, glossy foliage topped in early summer by the dramatic, spurred flowers that are perfect for bouquets. Taller varieties form an incredible backdrop for perennial plantings and all types look at home in both formal and informal beds.

Plant them in full sun in an area sheltered from strong winds.

Milkweed

Milkweed and Butterfly Weed plants, both members of the Asclepias family, are the sole food source for Monarch butterfly caterpillars. Planting a block of milkweed is the easiest way to help rebound the plummeting population of this beloved butterfly, but you might choose to plant it based on looks alone! With its saturated punch of color and constant line of visiting pollinators, this native plant has become immensely popular in perennial gardens nationwide. Choose flaming orange Butterfly Weed, the most drought tolerant of all the milkweeds, to thrive in your garden's driest spots, or plant Swamp Milkweed in moister areas.

Peony

Peonies produce colossal flowers atop masses of glossy green foliage, and require almost no care. In fact, many perennial peonies live over 100 years without any special effort from the gardener. That longevity comes with only one request: access to full sun and good soil. Popular in flower arrangements, these fragrant show-offs will last even longer if you can manage to trim their stems at an angle and change the vase water every other day.

Salvia

Heat-loving Salvias produce blooms in a wide range of color choices on upright spires. Their fragrant flowers and foliage attract many species of pollinators and also work to repel deer. Often called "Blue Sage," salvias like the favorite, 'May Night' have become major colormakers in perennial gardens from coast to coast.

Sedum

The common name for these beautiful plants is "Stonecrop" but it's not used much these days. In fact, most people now call the sedums "Sedum," and it's all due to one spectacular plant - the pink-blooming butterfly magnet 'Autumn Joy' Sedum, one of the most popular perennials of all time. Now available in a host of colors, sedums are succulents, whose thick, moisture-storing leaves help them perform best in full sun and arid, rocky soil.

Shrubs

Low maintenance and easy to grow, shrubs can be used to hide unsightly views, add privacy and buffer noise on tight properties, and can help divide your yard into garden "rooms". They can also provide cover for birds and other wildlife. Shrubs add height, create focal points and add year-round interest to the landscape. Spectacular new colors and features like variegated foliage make today's hardy shrubs great investments for your garden.

Bulbs

Pick the Right Spot

Even healthy bulbs will fail if they're planted in the wrong spot. Most bulbs do best in full sun (at least 6 hours of direct sun a day) and well-drained soil.

Get the Timing Right

When to plant bulbs depends on when they bloom. Spring-blooming bulbs, such as tulips and daffodils, should be planted in September or October when the soil temperatures have cooled. Summer-blooming beauties such as dahlia and gladiolus are best planted in the spring after all danger of frost has passed.

Plant Them Deep Enough

Not sure how deep to plant your bulbs? You're not alone—it's a very common question for gardeners. Generally, dig a hole two to three times deeper than the bulb is tall. So if you have a 3-inch-tall bulb, dig a hole 6 to 9 inches deep. There are always exceptions, so check the planting directions that come with the bulbs for more information.

Give Them Good Soil

Like most plants, bulbs appreciate well-drained soil rich in organic matter. So mix compost into your bulbs' planting holes to ensure good blooming. This is especially important if you have heavy clay soil or ground that stays wet.

Stop Weeds

Besides being just plain ugly, weeds steal nutrients from the soil and may attract insects or disease. The easiest way to prevent weeds from being an issue is to spread 2 to 3 inches of mulch over the soil. Your bulbs will easily push up through it, but most weed seeds won't.

Water Well

Bulbs are plants, too, so they appreciate a good drink after you plant them. This will encourage them to send out roots and become established more quickly. A good watering will eliminate air pockets in the soil that could cause your bulbs to dry out, too

Protect Your Investment

Critters such as squirrels love digging up freshly planted bulbs. Spread a layer of mulch to hide your bulb holes. If that doesn't help, weigh down a piece of mesh or chicken wire over the soil to keep critters from digging. It should be safe to remove the protective mesh or wire after the bulbs start to sprout out of the ground.

Make it Easy

If you live in a cold-winter climate and you want to save your tender summer bulbs, you'll need to store them in a frost-free place over the winter. An easy way to do this is to plant the bulbs in containers, then sink those containers in the ground. At the end of the season, simply dig up the containers and store them in a garage, basement, or shed that stays about 40 to 55 degrees.

Most bulbs look best when planted in big, irregular groupings (the more bulbs, the bigger the impact) instead of straight rows. So try tossing them onto the ground and plant them where they fall—it's fine if some bulbs end up being a little closer to each other than the recommended spacing. It adds to the natural look.

Crocosmia flowers

One of the best ways to break your garden out of the summer doldrums is to plant colorful summer-blooming bulbs and tubers, such as gladioli and tuberous begonias. Typically planted in the spring, these warm-weather bloomers usually don't survive cold winters if the bulbs are left in the ground. However, one notable exception is Crocosmia.

Despite its tropical origin, this vigorous perennial is hardy down to zone 5 and can stay in the ground year-round in all but the harshest climates, reliably blooming season after season. The lily-like flowers—in blazingly bright shades of red, orange and yellow—light up summer garden beds and borders and are especially irresistible to hummingbirds. Even when Crocosmia are not in bloom, their fountain-shaped clumps of spiky foliage offer contrasting form and vertical interest.

Botanical name:

Crocosmia; derived from the Greek words krokos (saffron) and osme (smell) because the dried flowers smell similar to saffron when steeped in water. Cultivars labeled as Crocosmia x crocosmiiflora are hybrids of multiple wild Crocosmia species.

Common names:

Montbretia, coppertips, falling stars

Plant type:

Herbaceous perennial, grown from clump-forming corms

Zones:

Use as a perennial in zones 5-9. In colder climates, you may need to lift the corms in the fall and store them indoors over winter.

Height:

1½ to 4 feet, depending on the variety

Exposure:

Thrives in full sun but also grows well in partial shade, although it may not flower as prolifically.

Bloom Time:

Mid to late summer

Color and characteristics:

Like Gladiolus, Crocosmia are members of the iris family (Iridaceae) and have similar swordlike foliage and flowers that open in succession from the bottom up. The trumpet-shaped blooms are lined up in rows along arching flower stalks and have prominent stamens and stigmas that flare out well beyond the petals. Although the color palette is limited to various shades of yellow, orange, and red, some cultivars are enhanced by attractive throat markings.

Special attributes:

• Attracts hummingbirds and butterflies

• Deer and rabbit resistant

• Excellent for cutting

• Naturalizes readily

PLANTING

When to plant:

In spring, after the danger of frost has passed. Crocosmia can be slow to sprout, especially if temperatures are cool. To jumpstart growth, wait until soil and air temperatures warm up.

How to plant:

In garden beds, plant the corms 2 to 3 inches deep and 8 to 10 inches apart, with the pointed end facing up. Mass the corms together in groups of 10 or more for the best effect. If growing in containers, plant to the same depth in any well-drained good-quality potting mix in a pot with adequate drainage holes. Learn more about planting and caring for bulbs.

Soil:

Prefers moist, well-drained, humus-rich soil. Avoid planting in heavy clays or soggy sites.

CARE

Watering:

Water as needed during the growing season to keep the soil evenly moist, giving your plants about an inch of water weekly.

Fertilizing:

Feed after initial planting or in early spring with a balanced slow-release fertilizer formulated for bulbs and tubers.

After blooming:

Crocosmia are self-cleaning and once the flowers are spent, they will simply fall off, giving way to attractive seedpods that persist into fall. After blooming is over, leave the foliage in place so it can gather sunlight to nourish next year's growth. When the leaves die back naturally late in the fall, you can cut them back to an inch or two above ground level.

Dividing:

Crocosmia multiplies enthusiastically and should be divided every 2 to 3 years to prevent overcrowding and to keep them vigorous. The plant develops cormlets along its roots, making it very easy to propagate. With a gentle twist, simply break apart the offsets you find attached to the base of the main corm and replant them. You can lift and divide congested clumps in fall or in the spring before new growth starts.

Winter protection:

Because Crocosmia are more cold-hardy than Gladiolus, you can usually leave the corms to overwinter in the ground without having to dig them up. To help ensure their survival, cover them with a layer of mulch to insulate them from severe cold snaps. If you live in zone 4 or below, don't take chances. Lift the corms and store them in a cool, dry location over winter and replant them in the spring.

Diseases and Pests:

Although impervious to most pests and diseases, crocosmias are particularly susceptible to spider mites. Avoid an infestation by hosing the leaves down with a spray of water once or twice a week.

This will dislodge any mites and create an inhospitable environment.

Amaryllis

With their ability to produce large, vibrantly colored blooms indoors in the depths of winter, amaryllis rivals the poinsettia as one of the most popular holiday flowers. The spectacular trumpet-shaped blooms brighten the dreariest day and instantly banish the winter doldrums. And depending on when you plant it, amaryllis can actually flower through early spring, enhancing your home with its floral beauty until the outdoor planting season arrives.

Not only are these breathtaking plants easy to grow, they will often rebloom year after year. "One amaryllis lights up a room; a group of three or more creates a spectacular display. Yet for all the floral pyrotechnics they deliver, these blooms are simple to cultivate and will, given proper care, provide multiple years of pleasure

Botanical name:

Hippeastrum

Plant type:

A tropical bulb, native to South America.

When to plant:

October until the end of April. It usually takes six to eight weeks for amaryllis to bloom, so for New Year's showstoppers, plant the bulbs in November. If you want the lily-like blooms in time for Easter, plant in February.

Flowering period:

7 to 10 weeks

Height:

12 to 36 inches

Flower size:

Six to 10 inches across, usually produced three or four per stem.

Colors/varieties:

You'll typically find amaryllis in various shades of red, white, pink, peach, or apricot, but there are also many striped, multicolored, and picotee selections. More recent introductions include double-flowered and dwarf varieties.

Precautions:

All parts of the plant can be toxic if ingested, especially the bulb. Keep away from children and pets.

How to grow
Planting:

Place the bulb in potting mix pointed side up, with its "neck" and "shoulders" above the soil surface. Place in a warm, well-lit spot (such as a south-facing window) until the bulb sprouts. Growth generally begins in two to eight weeks. To enjoy a continuous season of bloom—from the winter holidays until early spring—Ockenga suggests staggering your bulb planting by storing some bulbs in a cool, dry place, such as a basement or garage, and bringing them out of their slumber a few at a time.

Container:

Choose a heavy pot, such as clay or ceramic, to counterbalance the weight of the large flowers. Amaryllis bloom best when they are pot-bound, so the container should only be an inch or two wider than the diameter of the bulb. Once your plant takes off, a support stake may be needed to hold the blooms upright, especially for long-stemmed varieties.

Soil:

Average potting soil works fine, but the addition of perlite or sand will help to improve drainage and prevent soggy soil.

Water:

Give the bulb a good watering at planting time, and then water sparingly until growth starts. Overwatering when you first pot an amaryllis can cause bulb rot and poor root development. After the plant begins to develop foliage, keep the soil slightly moist. Watering once a week should be sufficient, depending on the heat and humidity in your home.

Lighting/temperature:

Since amaryllis are native to the tropics, warmth and sunlight will encourage them to break dormancy. Place newly potted bulbs in a brightly lit room at 65° to 75° F. Once they begin blooming, move them out of direct sunlight and into a cooler location to prolong the blooming period. Turn the pot a little every day to prevent your plant from leaning toward the light source.

Fertilizer:

A healthy amaryllis bulb contains all the nutrients it needs to bloom. But if you plan to keep your plant for reblooming next year, feed it regularly with a water-soluble houseplant fertilizer.

Growing in water:

It's also possible to grow an amaryllis in water in a clear glass container, to show off the beauty of the entire bulb. Nestle the roots around a base of pebbles and keep the water level no higher than the base of the bulb, changing it periodically. Be aware that this growing method can deplete the bulb's reserves, so it may take several years for the plant to bloom again.

Growing outdoors:

In frost-free areas of the South and West (Zones 8-10), amaryllis can be grown outdoors in the garden as perennials. Plant the bulbs in early fall for blooms the following spring. The bulbs can stay in the ground untended, where they will continue to re-flower and multiply for years to come.

Aftercare:

After all the flowers have faded, remove the stalks but leave the foliage intact. It will produce the fuel the bulb needs to flower again next year. With proper care, an amaryllis bulb can last for decades, but it needs a period of rest to replenish its resources

Gladiolus flowers

Gladioli are a gold standard in the florist trade, but they are so easy and economical to grow at home that any gardener can enjoy these showy blossoms. Avid glad fans often fill entire rows or garden beds with these colorful corms for the sole purpose of growing them for bouquets. But if the tender glads bred for cut flowers are too flamboyant for your tastes, try one of the resilient winter-hardy varieties, which are equally lovely and can remain outside year-round. Whether you wish to fill a vase with magnificent cut flowers or to keep your glads in the garden among other perennials, you'll find a range of striking varieties in nearly every color of the rainbow.

Botanical name:

Gladiolus xhortulanus

Common names:

Common gladiolus, garden glad, and sword lily (because of the long, pointed leaves)

Zones:

Perennial in zones 8-10. Can be grown as annuals in zones 2-7. Some G. nanus types are hardy to zone 4 or 5.

How they grow:

Although you will often see glads labeled as "summer bulbs," they are herbaceous perennials that grow from bulb-like corms covered with a fibrous papery skin. Unlike spring bulbs, glad corms are sensitive to freezing temperatures and must be dug up in fall and stored until planting time the following spring. In mild climates, some hardier glad hybrids can be left in the ground over winter.

Types:

You'll find countless cultivars of glads in local garden centers and catalogs, all derived from various combinations of more than 250 species, most of which are native to southern and central Africa and Eurasia.

The three main glad groups are:

• Grandiflora: The largest group of garden cultivars. These hybrids are the showiest of the bunch, with blooms up to 6 inches wide and the most extensive range of colors.

• Nanus: Another group commonly grown in the garden. Miniature hybrids that tend to be more cold-tolerant than their taller cousins.

• Primulinus: Have daintier hooded flowers and very narrow leaves.

Flower characteristics:

Most garden glads come in nearly any color and shade (except for true blue) in both solid and multicolored forms. Depending on the cultivar, the petals may be frilly, ruffled, semi-ruffled or plain, and the size can range from miniature (under 2 ½ inches in diameter) to gigantic (over 5 inches). The flowers are typically arranged on only one side of the stem and open in succession from the bottom up, with the largest flower at the base. As a bonus, hummingbirds really love these flowers!

Height:

1 to 5 feet

Bloom time:

From early summer until frost, depending on the cultivar and when the corms are planted.

Displaying glads

• Generally, glads are long-lasting cut flowers and will remain attractive for at least a week in a vase, but for the greatest longevity cut the stems when only a few flowers are open at the bottom the spike. The rest of the florets will open gradually over the next few days. As they do, pull off the bottom florets when they fade.

• Cut your glads in the early morning or late evening, when the temperatures are coolest and the stems are well hydrated. If you plan to store and replant your corms, don't be tempted to cut off all the foliage along with the flowers. Leave as many leaves as possible on the plant to help nourish the corm for the following spring.

• Although glads look stunning arranged in a tall vase, you can cut the blooms from the stems and arrange them in a shallow vase or bowl to make an attractive, low-profile centerpiece for a dining room table.

Hyacinth flowers

Hyacinths are one of the easiest spring bulbs to grow. Although hyacinth plants are small, they pack a big punch of both color and fragrance in their clusters of blooms. There are many varieties available in several colors, including purple, white, yellow and pink. Hyacinth bulbs can be grown indoors as well as in your garden.

Zones:

Generally 3-9, with some winter protection needed in zones lower than 5 and pre-chilling in fall required in zones higher than 7. (For tips on pre-chilling, see When to Plant in Care Tab)

Height/Spread:

6 inches to 1 foot tall, 3 to 6 inches wide

Exposure:

Full sun to light shade

Bloom Time:

March - April

Flower Color and Shape:

Single, double and multiflora blooms in shades of white, peach, orange, salmon, yellow, pink, red, purple, lavender, and blue.

Attracts:

Butterflies

Here are some ways to incorporate hyacinth flowers into your garden:

• Due to their small size, hyacinths are best planted in groups in beds, borders, or rock gardens.

• Their small shape and spiky stalks mix well with other spring bulbs, providing contrast to taller tulips and daffodils.

• Plant them near walkways, entries, or patios to enjoy their scent.

• Container planting is also ideal due to their compact size. They can be planted closer together in a pot - almost touching, as they do not need room to spread.

• Plant them in pots outdoors and then bring inside just before blooming to provide a natural, indoor air freshener.

Snowdrops

The sight of snowdrop shoots poking up through snow-covered ground is one of the first signs that spring is near. It was once thought that their leaves were thermogenic, producing their own heat in order to melt through the snow. However, it is more likely a thermal effect of sunlight heating the tips of the leaves warmer than the surrounding snow. Each bulb produces 2-3 narrow leaves and a single flower scape (or stalk)

Zones:

3-9, varies by species and cultivar.

Height/Spread:

Varieties range 6-12 inches tall.

Exposure:

Full sun to light shade.

Bloom Time:

February-April

Flower Color and Size:

Small, bell-shaped, fragrant, white flowers with green tips or markings. Each flower consists of two whorls of three lobes.

Other:

Attracts pollinators.

Planting snowdrops

When to plant:

Plant dormant snowdrop bulbs in fall. Planting in the green can be done in the spring after flowering.

Where to plant:

Snowdrops do well under late-leafing deciduous trees that allow sunlight to the snowdrop's leaves while they are growing in early spring. Evergreens do not allow enough spring sunlight through for snowdrops to grow well.

How to plant:

Plant snowdrop bulbs 2-3 inches deep, approximately 3 inches apart, with their points up. Water well to settle the soil.

Other:

It is recommended to wear gloves when planting snowdrops to avoid possible skin irritation

Caring for snowdrops

Soil

Moist, humus-rich, well-drained soil.

Amendments & Fertilizer:

Wild-growing snowdrops fend for themselves quite well, but if they are growing in planter beds or containers, they will benefit from a potassium-rich fertilizer. This should be applied every 7-10 days from the time foliage appears until it begins to yellow and wilt. A mulch of compost in autumn can also help nourish the growing bulbs.

Watering:

Light to moderate water. Soil should remain moist throughout the growing season.

Propagation:

Snowdrop bulbs will multiply and naturalize if left in an area undisturbed. They are easily dug up, divided and transplanted. Dig them up any time after the foliage has died back in mid-to-late spring until early autumn. Galanthus bulbs tend to dry out if left out of the ground, so re-plant immediately. By mid-autumn, they will have started growing again and shouldn't be disturbed until after blooming.

Diseases and Pests:

There are no serious disease or pest problems. Snowdrops are also deer resistant.

Other:

After blooming, allow the leaves to remain in place to gather and store energy for next year. Snowdrops will take a year to get established. In their second year, they will produce more flowers and begin to multiply and spread.

Deer-proof bulbs

Random bulb genera that deer ignore include Canna, Oxalis and Cyclamen. Many more deer-proof bulbs may be found in the Amaryllis family. Poisonous, and seemingly immune to browsing by deer, these include all daffodils (Narcissus), all snowdrops (Galanthus) and all Leucojum, including both spring and summer snowflakes. All three genera thrive in Maine, Massachusetts, Minnesota and Michigan, as well as states farther south.

Gardeners in California and similar Mediterranean regions can grow Amaryllis belladona, the true amaryllis, commonly known as naked lady. Other tender Amaryllis family members include Crinum,

Hippeastrum, Nerine, Zephyranthes and another naked lady, also known as surprise lily or magic lily, Lycoris species and cultivars, popular with gardeners in North and South Carolina, Tennessee, Mississippi and any other Zone 9 to 11 region you care to name

Aroids (plants in the Araceae or Arum family) contain oxalic acid crystals in all parts of the plants. Accordingly, all jack-in-the-pulpit (Arisaema species), whether native North American or exotic Asian, are distasteful to deer. So are caladium, seasonal plants for cooler climates and permanent features in Florida gardens. Deer in the Gulf states, Florida and the Texas Gulf region also decline to dine on calla lily, Calla and Zantedeschia species and cultivars.

Though Lily family bulbs such as lilies and tulips are popular salad bar favorites for deer, there are a few bulbs in this family that they ignore. These include all the ornamental onions (Allium species and cultivars) every Camassia I ever planted; and the pretty little blue-flowered glory of the snow (Chionodoxa). Spring-flowering squills (Scilla) are also unharmed. Every fritillaria, from the stately but skunk-smelling crown imperial (Fritillaria imperialis) to the charming checkered bell flowers of Guinea hen flower (F. meleagris), are also left alone. Grape hyacinths (Muscari species and cultivars) grow and flower unhindered. Confusingly called naked lady (which seems a popular name) or fall crocus (which it is not), the poisonous fall-flowering Colchicum remains unmolested. Though hyacinths do poorly in subsequent years, deer don't eat them and so cannot be the culprits for their decline in my garden. Deer will, however, occasionally chew the tips off leaves of wood hyacinth (Hyacinthoides hispanica).

So even if tulips are devoured and dahlias gobbled down, take heart. There are lumpy underground treasures that you can plant with confidence and enjoy.

Planting and storing flower bulbs

Bulbs are little packets of flower power that make us wait weeks, sometimes months, for results, are they worth it. The term "bulb" often refers not only to true bulbs, but also plants with tuberous roots, tubers, corms, and rhizomes; the information here can be applied to all of these. With a little basic knowledge, anyone can grow beautiful bulbs.

Types of bulbs

Bulbs can be separated into two main types: spring and summer.

Spring bulbs: Also called hardy bulbs, these bulbs are planted in fall, spend winter in the ground, and flower in spring. Some of the more common spring bulbs are tulips, irises, daffodils, hyacinth, allium and crocus. These bulbs need several weeks of cold temperatures to break their dormancy and flower to their full potential.

Summer bulbs: Also called tender bulbs, these bulbs are planted in spring and flower or leaf out in summer. Gladiolus, lilies, caladiums, and elephant ears are common examples of summer bulbs. Some will bloom later in summer or for a longer time, like dahlias that bloom into fall. Summer bulbs aren't tolerant of cold temperatures and are planted only after the ground warms up and there's no longer a threat of frost. If purchased before planting time, store them in a cool, dry spot until planting.

Planting bulbs

When to plant bulbs

Zones 4 to 7: In colder climates, spring bulbs can be planted as soon as the ground is cool, evening temperatures average 40° to 50°F, and it is at least 6 to 8 weeks before the ground freezes. If timed right, this should be as soon as possible after purchase. However, bulbs can be stored in the refrigerator if needed until planting. (See Helpful Hints below for more information on storing bulbs in the refrigerator.) Summer bulbs should be planted in mid to late spring.

Zones 8 to 10: In warmer climates, spring bulbs will need to be chilled in the refrigerator for 6 to 10 weeks (depending on the bulb) until the ground cools enough for planting. (See Helpful Hints below for more information on storing bulbs in the refrigerator.) Summer bulbs can be planted early to mid-spring.

Average planting times for spring bulbs:

• September to October — Zones 4 and 5

• October to early November — Zones 6 and 7

• November to early December — Zones 8 and 9

• Late December to early January — Zone 10

Average planting times for summer bulbs:

• Late March to May — Zones 8 to 10

• May to June — Zones 4 to 7

Where to plant bulbs

As long as you ensure that your bulbs have good drainage and sunlight, you can plant them just about anywhere. Drainage is critical to keep bulbs from rotting. They like loamy or slightly sandy soil because it provides the drainage and nutrients they need. Early-spring bloomers can be planted under deciduous trees where they'll get enough sun to bloom before the tree's leaves block it out. However, they'll only bloom well the first year, as they'll need sunlight later for the leaves to gather enough energy for the next year's bloom.

Plan before you plant

Bulbs can be grown in many ways — formal gardens, meadow gardens, scattered in lawns, under trees, or strategically planted throughout beds and borders. Many bulbs will naturalize in an area and multiply, coming back year after year, so plan carefully and you can have years of enjoyment from one planting.

• Plant in clusters for greater visual impact.

• Take into account bloom time — plant a combination of early, mid- and late-season bloomers to extend the season.

• Hide dying foliage of low-growing bulbs that are past their prime with taller bulbs planted in front or with companion plants.

• Layer plant heights from front to back when planting varieties that will bloom at the same time.

• Many bulbs are perfect for container planting — bring them into view when blooming and move out of the way when foliage is wilting and when dormant. Plant closer together in containers than specified for in-ground planting.

• Bulbs can provide bright, vibrant color — think about how those colors will blend with their surroundings.

• Companion plants keep the planting area going when bulbs are dormant. Some good perennial companions are sedum, coreopsis, thyme, cranesbill, daylilies, coral bells, brunnera, hosta, hellebores, or bleeding heart.

How to plant bulbs

Bulbs can be planted in layers by digging up an entire area down to the proper depth, placing the bulbs and covering; or in individual holes dug for each bulb. Individual planting is made easier with a bedding plant auger

1. Determine the planting depth for the type of bulb you're planting. Depth is important for bulbs. If planted too deep, they will bloom late or not at all. If planted too shallow, new growth may become exposed too soon and risk damage by cold temperatures. If you are unsure of the exact planting depth, a good general rule of thumb is to plant the bulb 2 to 3 times as deep as the bulb is tall.

2. Prepare the soil by loosening and mixing in organic material if needed for added nutrients or to improve drainage. Special bulb fertilizer can be added; follow the package directions.

3. Place the bulbs with the pointy-end up and with the roots down. If you're not sure of the top or bottom

of the bulb, plant it on its side and it will find its way to the surface.

4. Cover with soil and a light layer of mulch.

5. Newly planted bulbs should be watered well to get settled in.

6. If needed, protect bulbs from critters by staking down wire mesh or chicken wire over the beds or planting them in bulb baskets or wire cages.

Digging up bulbs

• Cut any remaining stems and foliage back to a couple inches above the soil level.

• Loosen the soil around the bulbs carefully and remove them.

• Shake as much soil as possible from the bulb and roots.

• Spread them out on newspaper in a cool, shady place and allow them to dry for a few days. Make sure they are out of reach of animals and children as some bulbs are poisonous.

• Store in an aerated paper or mesh bag or cardboard box with holes. You can add slightly damp vermiculite or perlite so they don't dry out too much.

• Store in a cool, dark, and dry location with temperatures 50 to 60 degrees, such as a basement or garage.

• Check bulbs monthly for any signs of mold or rot.

Helpful hints

• Don't store fruit (especially apples) or vegetables in the refrigerator at the same time bulbs are being stored or pre-chilled. They emit ethylene gas that can kill the plant inside the bulb.

• Soil pH of 6 to 7 brings out better color in blooming bulb flowers.

• Plant bulbs in the same season they are purchased, they won't last until next year.

• If bulbs are to be left in the ground while dormant, place a marker so that you remember where they are after you've cut the foliage back.

• Bulbs need to breathe, so store them in aerated paper or mesh bags, never in plastic.

Buying bulbs

Here are a few tips to help you pick the best bulbs:

• Bulbs should feel firm to the touch, not soft or spongy.

• Choose bulbs that don't have any signs of disease, mold, or severe damage.

• At the time of purchase, bulbs should show little or no root growth or sprouting. Lilies are an exception, as they often have fleshy roots attached.

• The old saying, you get what you pay for, holds true with bulbs. Quality bulbs will make the difference between lackluster blooming and an impressive show.

CONCLUSION

For all bulbs, after blooming, cut only the flower stem back. Leave foliage intact until it turns yellow and wilts to the ground; the leaves are gathering and storing energy for next year. If the foliage is cut back too soon, bulbs may not perform well—or at all—the following year. Spring bulbs: In warmer climates bulbs that require chilling can be dug up and stored until pre-chilling time the following fall. For colder climates, they can stay in the ground. Many will multiply and return year after year. Summer bulbs: In warmer climates, bulbs can be left in the ground with a layer of mulch in winter to protect and insulate them. In colder climates, they'll need to be dug up and stored until the following spring.

Annual plant cycle is in reference to a once a year cycle of life. Annual garden plants germinate from seed, then blossom and finally set seeds before dying back. Although they die back and must be replanted each year, they are generally showier than perennial plants with a long bloom period from spring to just before the first fall frost. The above is the simplest explanation as to what an annual plant is; however, the answer begins to get complicated with the following information. Some annual garden plants are referred to as hardy annuals or half-hardy annuals, while even some perennials may be grown as annuals.

www.ingramcontent.com/pod-product-compliance
Lightning Source LLC
Chambersburg PA
CBHW071545150726
48000CB00002B/951